# The History

# From Sigiriya to Serendipity

# Land of Legends: The Enchanting Origins of Sri Lanka

Sri Lanka, a captivating island nestled in the Indian Ocean, has a rich and fascinating history that dates back thousands of years. Known as "The Pearl of the Indian Ocean," it has been a land of legends, shrouded in myth and folklore, where reality intertwines with the realm of imagination.

The origins of Sri Lanka are deeply rooted in ancient times. Archeological evidence suggests that the island was inhabited as early as the Paleolithic era, around 125,000 years ago. The early settlers were believed to be hunter-gatherer communities, living off the bountiful resources provided by the lush forests and abundant wildlife.

One of the most intriguing legends surrounding the origins of Sri Lanka is the tale of Prince Vijaya. According to ancient chronicles, Prince Vijaya, an exiled prince from northern India, arrived on the island around the 6th century BCE. He is said to have established the first organized civilization, known as the Sinhalese, in what is now present-day Sri Lanka. This legend forms the foundation of the Sinhalese people's cultural identity, as they trace their ancestry back to Prince Vijaya.

The island's strategic location in the ancient maritime trade routes made it a melting pot of different cultures and civilizations. Traders from ancient Persia, Arabia, India, and China frequented Sri Lanka, leaving indelible imprints on its history. The island became a vibrant hub of cultural exchange and a coveted destination for traders seeking exotic goods, such as spices, gems, and precious metals.

Buddhism, one of the most influential religions in Sri Lanka, arrived during the reign of Emperor Ashoka in the 3rd century BCE. Ashoka, a powerful Indian ruler, sent his son Mahinda to introduce Buddhism to the island. This event marked a pivotal moment in Sri Lankan history, as Buddhism became the dominant religion, shaping the island's spiritual and cultural landscape.

The ancient cities of Anuradhapura and Polonnaruwa played vital roles in Sri Lanka's history. Anuradhapura, founded in the 4th century BCE, served as the capital of the Sinhalese kingdom for over a millennium. It flourished as a center of Buddhism and was adorned with magnificent stupas, palaces, and monasteries. Polonnaruwa, established in the 10th century CE, succeeded Anuradhapura as the capital and witnessed the architectural and artistic zenith of Sri Lanka's medieval period.

The island's history also bears witness to the influence of the Chola dynasty of South India. The Cholas embarked on several military campaigns, resulting in the temporary annexation of Sri Lanka. Their rule left an enduring impact on the island's political and cultural landscape, with Tamil influences permeating various aspects of Sri Lankan society.

The arrival of European powers in the 16th century marked a new chapter in Sri Lanka's history. The Portuguese, led by explorer Vasco da Gama, were the first to establish a presence on the island. They sought to control the lucrative spice trade and gradually gained control over coastal regions, imposing their authority on local kingdoms.

The Dutch, who succeeded the Portuguese, established a strong foothold in Sri Lanka during the 17th century. They seized control of major ports and implemented a system of governance that significantly impacted the island's social and economic structure. The Dutch East India Company, known as the VOC, introduced new crops like coffee and cinnamon, which transformed Sri Lanka into a prosperous plantation economy.

The British arrived in Sri Lanka in the late 18th century, during a time when the Dutch influence was waning. The British East India Company gradually expanded its control, ultimately leading to the island becoming a crown colony in 1802. British colonial rule had a profound and lasting impact on Sri Lanka, shaping its modern institutions, infrastructure, and social dynamics.

The quest for independence and self-governance gained momentum in the 20th century, fueled by a growing sense of national identity among the Sri Lankan people. The struggle for independence culminated in 1948 when Sri Lanka finally gained its sovereignty. However, the aftermath of independence was marred by ethnic tensions and political challenges that would shape the country's trajectory in the coming decades.

Sri Lanka's enchanting origins are not limited to its human history. The island's abundant wildlife and diverse ecosystems have captivated the imaginations of nature enthusiasts. From the majestic elephants that roam its national parks to the elusive leopards of Yala, Sri Lanka's wildlife is a treasure trove of biodiversity. It is home to a multitude of endemic species, making conservation efforts of utmost importance to preserve this natural heritage.

As we delve deeper into the history of Sri Lanka, we uncover a tapestry of legends, cultures, and civilizations that have left an indelible mark on this enchanting island. From ancient origins to modern-day developments, Sri Lanka's story is one of resilience, diversity, and the enduring spirit of its people.

# Ancient Ceylon: The Early Settlements and Indigenous Cultures

Ancient Ceylon, known today as Sri Lanka, holds a captivating history that stretches back millennia. It was a land where early settlements and indigenous cultures flourished, leaving behind traces of their existence and shaping the foundation of Sri Lanka's rich heritage.

The story of ancient Ceylon begins in the prehistoric era, with evidence of human habitation dating as far back as the Paleolithic period, approximately 125,000 years ago. These early settlers, believed to be hunter-gatherer communities, roamed the island's lush forests and coastal regions, relying on its abundant natural resources for sustenance.

As time passed, these early hunter-gatherer societies evolved, giving rise to the first agricultural communities in Sri Lanka. The advent of agriculture brought about significant changes in the lifestyle of the island's inhabitants. They began cultivating crops such as rice, millet, and barley, allowing for settled communities to emerge.

One of the remarkable aspects of ancient Ceylon was its geographical location, strategically positioned in the Indian Ocean. This advantageous position made it a focal point for maritime trade, attracting merchants and explorers from distant lands. The island became a melting pot of cultures, as traders from India, Arabia, Persia, and China visited its shores, engaging in commercial activities and cultural exchange.

Archaeological excavations have unearthed evidence of early settlements and urban centers that thrived in ancient Ceylon. Among the most notable sites is Anuradhapura, founded around the 4th century BCE. Anuradhapura served as the capital of the Sinhalese kingdom for over a millennium, encompassing a glorious period of architectural, artistic, and religious achievements.

The indigenous cultures of ancient Ceylon developed distinct social and political systems. The island was divided into numerous principalities or kingdoms, each governed by a local ruler known as a "maharaja." These principalities often engaged in alliances, conflicts, and territorial disputes, shaping the complex political landscape of the time.

Religion played a significant role in the lives of ancient Sri Lankans. Even before the arrival of Buddhism, indigenous beliefs and practices prevailed. These early religions were rooted in animism and worship of natural forces. Rituals were conducted to appease deities associated with fertility, harvest, and protection. Ancient rituals and ceremonies showcased the reverence the early Sri Lankans held for their spiritual beliefs.

The introduction of Buddhism in the 3rd century BCE by Emperor Ashoka's emissary, Mahinda, transformed the religious landscape of ancient Ceylon. Buddhism took root and flourished, becoming the predominant religion on the island. Monastic communities, or "sanghas," were established, and Buddhist doctrines and teachings became integral to the fabric of Sri Lankan society. Monasteries, stupas, and intricate rock-cut cave temples emerged as significant architectural expressions of the Buddhist influence.

The ancient Sri Lankans also left behind impressive irrigation systems that showcased their ingenuity and engineering prowess. Elaborate networks of reservoirs, canals, and tanks were constructed to manage and distribute water for agriculture. These sophisticated hydraulic structures, such as the colossal reservoirs at Anuradhapura, stand as a testament to the technological advancements of ancient Ceylon.

Trade and commerce played a crucial role in the ancient Sri Lankan economy. The island's strategic location facilitated maritime trade routes, connecting it to various regions in the Indian Ocean. Sri Lanka's valuable resources, including gems, spices, precious metals, and ivory, attracted merchants from across the seas. Traders exchanged goods, ideas, and cultural influences, fostering a cosmopolitan atmosphere in ancient Ceylon.

The ancient settlements and indigenous cultures of Ceylon form the bedrock of Sri Lanka's historical identity. Their achievements in agriculture, architecture, irrigation, and trade laid the foundation for the island's future developments. The cultural and technological legacies they left behind continue to inspire awe and admiration, reminding us of the ingenuity and resilience of ancient Ceylon's early inhabitants.

# Sigiriya: The Majestic Rock Fortress of King Kasyapa

Nestled amidst the dense jungles of Sri Lanka stands an architectural marvel that has captivated the world for centuries—Sigiriya, the majestic rock fortress of King Kasyapa. Rising abruptly from the surrounding plains, this UNESCO World Heritage site has not only mesmerized visitors with its awe-inspiring beauty but has also held secrets and stories of a bygone era.

Sigiriya, also known as the Lion Rock, is situated in the central Matale District of Sri Lanka. Its history dates back to the 5th century CE, during the reign of King Kasyapa, a complex and enigmatic figure in Sri Lankan history. The construction of Sigiriya is believed to have been a grand statement of his power, wealth, and ambition.

The fortress is built on a massive column of rock, reaching a height of over 200 meters (660 feet). The rock itself is a geological marvel, composed of hardened magma from an extinct volcano. Its sheer vertical walls, adorned with intricate frescoes, lead visitors to marvel at the ingenuity and engineering skills of the ancient Sri Lankans.

To reach the summit, visitors must pass through a series of magnificent and elaborate entranceways. The most iconic among them is the Lion Gate, an imposing stone structure featuring the remnants of two enormous lion paws. Historians believe that an entire lion figure once stood at the entrance, serving as a symbol of the king's power and authority.

As visitors ascend the rock, they encounter a fascinating network of landscaped gardens, water gardens, and terraced platforms. These gardens were meticulously designed, incorporating water features, fountains, and even a sophisticated irrigation system. The water gardens, with their symmetrically arranged ponds and channels, showcase the mastery of hydraulic engineering achieved by the ancient Sri Lankans.

One of the most remarkable features of Sigiriya is the collection of frescoes adorning a sheltered rock ledge on the western face. These paintings depict celestial maidens, known as "Apsaras," with their ethereal beauty and vibrant colors. The frescoes are not only aesthetically captivating but also offer insights into the artistic skills and cultural practices of ancient Sri Lanka.

Upon reaching the summit of Sigiriya, visitors are rewarded with breathtaking panoramic views of the surrounding landscape. From this vantage point, the extent of King Kasyapa's vision becomes apparent. He sought to create an impregnable fortress that would not only serve as his residence but also convey his authority to all who beheld it.

Archaeological excavations on the summit have revealed evidence of the palace complex that once adorned the rock. The remnants of brick walls, water conduits, and foundations provide glimpses into the opulence and grandeur that once characterized this royal abode. The palace featured intricate architectural details, such as the famous Mirror Wall, which was once polished to a reflective surface, and the Cobra Hood Cave, an ingeniously designed cave with painted motifs resembling cobra hoods.

The exact circumstances surrounding the downfall of King Kasyapa and the subsequent abandonment of Sigiriya remain shrouded in mystery. Historical accounts suggest that after his defeat in a battle against his brother, King Kasyapa chose to take his own life rather than face capture. The rock fortress was subsequently abandoned and eventually reclaimed by the forces of nature.

Sigiriya's rediscovery in the early 19th century sparked a renewed fascination with its historical significance. Excavations, restoration efforts, and ongoing research continue to unravel the secrets of this ancient marvel. Sigiriya stands as a testament to the architectural brilliance, artistic finesse, and cultural richness of ancient Sri Lanka.

As visitors explore Sigiriya today, they are transported back in time, wandering the footsteps of kings and experiencing the awe-inspiring splendor that once graced this majestic rock fortress. Sigiriya's enduring allure reminds us of the enduring legacy of the ancient Sri Lankans and their ability to create enduring masterpieces that transcend the passage of time.

# The Arrival of Buddhism: The Transformative Influence of Emperor Ashoka

The advent of Buddhism in ancient Sri Lanka marked a significant turning point in its history, with the transformative influence of Emperor Ashoka resonating throughout the island. Ashoka, the great Mauryan emperor of India, played a pivotal role in spreading the teachings of Buddhism, leaving an indelible impact on Sri Lankan society, culture, and spirituality.

Emperor Ashoka ascended the throne in 269 BCE, inheriting an empire that had been forged through conquest and warfare. However, after a particularly brutal military campaign, Ashoka experienced a profound transformation. He embraced the principles of non-violence, compassion, and moral conduct, espoused by Buddhism, and sought to implement these values throughout his empire.

Ashoka's conversion to Buddhism had profound implications not only for India but also for neighboring regions, including Sri Lanka. He sent his son Mahinda, along with a group of Buddhist missionaries, to Sri Lanka with the noble mission of spreading the teachings of the Buddha. This significant event, known as the "Mahinda Mission," paved the way for the widespread adoption of Buddhism on the island.

Upon their arrival in Sri Lanka, Mahinda and the Buddhist missionaries encountered King Devanampiya Tissa, the ruler of the time. The king, influenced by the teachings of Mahinda, embraced Buddhism and subsequently extended his patronage and support to the newly introduced religion. The conversion of the king had a ripple effect throughout the kingdom, leading to the gradual acceptance and adoption of Buddhism by the Sri Lankan population.

The impact of Emperor Ashoka's influence on Sri Lanka was profound. The arrival of Buddhism brought about a radical shift in the religious and philosophical landscape of the island. Buddhist principles such as the Four Noble Truths, the Eightfold Path, and the practice of meditation resonated with the people, offering a path to enlightenment and liberation from suffering.

Buddhism became the guiding force in Sri Lankan society, influencing various aspects of life, including governance, art, architecture, and education. Monastic orders, known as "sanghas," were established, providing a framework for spiritual practice and community engagement. Buddhist monks, revered for their wisdom and ethical conduct, played a crucial role in disseminating the teachings and guiding the faithful.

The spread of Buddhism also led to the construction of magnificent religious monuments and monastic complexes throughout Sri Lanka. Stupas, or dagobas, became symbols of veneration, enshrining relics of the Buddha or revered Buddhist monks. These monumental structures, such as the Ruwanwelisaya in Anuradhapura and the Jetavanaramaya in Polonnaruwa, stood as testaments to the devotion and architectural prowess of the ancient Sri Lankans.

Art and literature flourished under the patronage of Buddhism. Intricate carvings, frescoes, and sculptures adorned temples and cave complexes, depicting scenes from the life of the Buddha, Jataka tales, and the Buddhist cosmology. The Sigiriya frescoes, showcasing celestial maidens, and the Aukana Buddha statue, standing tall and serene, exemplify the artistic expressions inspired by Buddhist beliefs.

Buddhism's influence extended beyond religion and aesthetics. It played a vital role in shaping the moral and ethical framework of Sri Lankan society. The emphasis on compassion, mindfulness, and the cultivation of virtuous qualities resonated with the people, influencing their interpersonal relationships, social interactions, and ethical decision-making.

The introduction of Buddhism also fostered scholarly pursuits and intellectual development. Monastic centers became centers of learning, where Buddhist monks engaged in scholarly activities, preserved sacred texts, and engaged in philosophical debates. The establishment of Buddhist universities, such as the ancient Mahavihara in Anuradhapura, promoted education and the dissemination of knowledge.

The transformative influence of Emperor Ashoka and the arrival of Buddhism in Sri Lanka brought about lasting changes in the island's cultural, social, and spiritual fabric. Buddhism became deeply ingrained in the consciousness of the Sri Lankan people, shaping their worldview, values, and way of life.

Today, Buddhism remains a significant influence in Sri Lanka, with countless temples, rituals, and practices keeping the flame of the Buddha's teachings alive. The profound impact of Emperor Ashoka's mission and the subsequent adoption of Buddhism continue to shape the identity and spiritual heritage of the island.

# Anuradhapura: The Glorious Capital of the Sinhalese Kingdom

Anuradhapura, the ancient capital of the Sinhalese kingdom, stands as a testament to the grandeur and splendor of Sri Lanka's historical past. Situated in the North Central Province of the island, Anuradhapura served as the political, religious, and cultural center of Sri Lanka for over a millennium. Its remarkable history, magnificent architecture, and religious significance have captured the imagination of visitors from around the world.

The origins of Anuradhapura can be traced back to the 4th century BCE when it was established by King Pandukabhaya. The city grew steadily in size and importance, becoming the capital of the Sinhalese kingdom. Over the centuries, successive kings expanded and embellished Anuradhapura, creating a cityscape that showcased their power, wealth, and devotion to Buddhism.

Anuradhapura's rise to prominence was closely intertwined with the spread of Buddhism on the island. The arrival of Emperor Ashoka's son, Mahinda, and the subsequent conversion of King Devanampiya Tissa in the 3rd century BCE marked a significant turning point. Buddhism became the state religion, and Anuradhapura became a center for Buddhist worship, scholarship, and pilgrimage.

The city's layout and architecture reflected its significance as a religious and administrative capital. The core of Anuradhapura was dominated by the sacred precincts, or "mahaviharas," which housed numerous monastic complexes, stupas, and other religious structures. The sacred Bodhi tree, a sapling brought from Bodh Gaya in India, became the centerpiece of the city and a revered object of veneration for Buddhists.

The monastic complexes, such as the Mahavihara and Abhayagiri, were centers of learning, where Buddhist monks engaged in scholarly pursuits, preserved sacred texts, and disseminated knowledge. These monastic communities attracted scholars, intellectuals, and pilgrims from across the Buddhist world, contributing to the city's intellectual and cultural vibrancy.

The stupas of Anuradhapura were monumental structures that enshrined relics of the Buddha or eminent Buddhist monks. The most famous among them is the Ruwanwelisaya, constructed by King Dutugemunu in the 2nd century BCE. It stands as a testament to the grandeur of Anuradhapura, with its vast dome, intricate carvings, and the devotion of countless pilgrims who continue to pay homage to this sacred site.

Anuradhapura's architectural wonders extended beyond stupas. Elaborate stone-carved moonstones, guard stones, and pillars adorned pathways and entranceways, showcasing the craftsmanship and artistic prowess of the ancient Sinhalese. The Abhayagiri Dagoba, the Jetavanaramaya, the Lovamahapaya (Brazen Palace), and the Samadhi Buddha statue are just a few examples of the architectural marvels that once graced the city.

Anuradhapura's influence was not limited to Sri Lanka alone. As a prominent center of Buddhism, it attracted pilgrims and scholars from far and wide. The city's fame spread across the Buddhist world, and its architectural and artistic styles influenced the development of Buddhist art and architecture in Southeast Asia.

Despite its glorious past, Anuradhapura's decline began in the 10th century CE due to repeated invasions, shifting political power, and the rise of new capitals. The city gradually fell into disuse and was eventually reclaimed by the surrounding jungle, becoming a hidden treasure awaiting rediscovery.

Anuradhapura's rediscovery in the 19th century sparked renewed interest in its historical significance. Archaeological excavations, conservation efforts, and ongoing research continue to unravel the mysteries and unravel the secrets of this ancient capital. Today, Anuradhapura stands as a UNESCO World Heritage Site, drawing visitors from around the world to explore its majestic ruins, relive its glorious past, and contemplate the spiritual heritage it embodies.

The legacy of Anuradhapura, the glorious capital of the Sinhalese kingdom, endures as a testament to the ingenuity, devotion, and cultural richness of ancient Sri Lanka. It stands as a symbol of the nation's historical identity, reminding us of the achievements and aspirations of the past.

# Polonnaruwa: The Resplendent City of King Parakramabahu

Polonnaruwa, an ancient city in Sri Lanka, stands as a testament to the architectural brilliance and cultural richness of the island's medieval period. Situated in the North Central Province, Polonnaruwa flourished as the capital of Sri Lanka from the 11th to the 13th centuries CE, under the reign of King Parakramabahu the Great. This resplendent city showcases the grandeur and achievements of a bygone era, leaving behind a remarkable legacy that continues to captivate visitors.

Polonnaruwa rose to prominence during the Chola invasions, a time when Sri Lanka faced external threats from the powerful Chola dynasty of South India. It was King Vijayabahu I who established Polonnaruwa as his capital in the 11th century CE, reclaiming Sri Lankan sovereignty and ushering in a new era of stability and cultural renaissance.

However, it was under the rule of King Parakramabahu the Great, who ascended the throne in 1153 CE, that Polonnaruwa reached its zenith. Known for his administrative acumen, military prowess, and patronage of the arts, King Parakramabahu embarked on an ambitious program of city planning, architectural projects, and cultural advancements that would shape the destiny of Polonnaruwa.

The city of Polonnaruwa was meticulously planned, featuring a grid-like layout with distinct zones dedicated to administrative, religious, and residential purposes. The

Royal Palace complex, positioned at the heart of the city, showcased the grandeur and opulence befitting a royal capital. Surrounding it were the royal gardens, exquisitely landscaped with ornamental ponds, pavilions, and flowering plants.

Religion played a central role in the life of Polonnaruwa. Buddhist monasteries and shrines, such as the Gal Vihara, Thuparama, and Lankatilaka, dotted the cityscape, offering spiritual solace and guidance to its inhabitants. These religious edifices housed magnificent statues, intricate carvings, and sacred relics, illustrating the devotion and artistic finesse of the medieval Sri Lankans.

Polonnaruwa's architectural wonders extended beyond religious structures. The city boasted remarkable engineering feats, including a sophisticated irrigation system that harnessed the waters of the Parakrama Samudra, a vast reservoir. This irrigation network facilitated agriculture, enabling the cultivation of rice and other crops, thereby ensuring the prosperity and sustenance of the city's inhabitants.

Art and culture flourished under King Parakramabahu's patronage. Polonnaruwa became a hub of artistic expression, with stone carvings, bronze sculptures, and intricate murals adorning temples and palaces. The famous Polonnaruwa Vatadage, a circular relic house, stands as a testament to the architectural mastery of the time.

Trade and commerce thrived in Polonnaruwa, with the city serving as a center for regional and international trade. The city's strategic location near major trade routes facilitated the exchange of goods, ideas, and cultural influences. Merchants from various parts of the world frequented

Polonnaruwa, bringing with them spices, gems, textiles, and other commodities.

Despite its grandeur, Polonnaruwa's glory was relatively short-lived. In the late 13th century, the city fell victim to repeated invasions, political instability, and changing power dynamics. It gradually declined, succumbing to nature's embrace and fading into obscurity.

Polonnaruwa's rediscovery in the 19th century sparked renewed interest in its historical significance. Archaeological excavations and ongoing preservation efforts have unearthed and restored the magnificent structures and artistic treasures of the city. Today, Polonnaruwa stands as a UNESCO World Heritage Site, attracting visitors from around the globe who seek to immerse themselves in the splendor and heritage of this medieval marvel.

The resplendent city of Polonnaruwa, crafted under the visionary leadership of King Parakramabahu the Great, stands as a testament to the ingenuity, artistic prowess, and cultural richness of medieval Sri Lanka. It invites us to marvel at the achievements of a bygone era and reflect upon the timeless beauty and wisdom that resonate from its ancient stones.

# Chola Conquests: Tamil Influence on Sri Lankan History

The history of Sri Lanka is a tapestry woven with diverse cultural influences, and one of the significant chapters in this narrative is the Chola conquests. The Chola dynasty, which emerged as a powerful force in South India during the medieval period, played a significant role in shaping Sri Lankan history and leaving a lasting Tamil influence on the island.

The Chola Empire, under the rule of emperors such as Rajendra Chola I and his successors, embarked on ambitious military campaigns that expanded their dominion far beyond the Indian subcontinent. The conquests of the Cholas brought them into contact with Sri Lanka, known at the time as Ceylon, and marked the beginning of a significant period of Tamil influence on the island.

The Chola conquest of Sri Lanka occurred in the 10th century CE. The ruler at the time, King Rajaraja Chola I, launched an invasion of the island, seeking to establish Chola authority and expand their maritime empire. The Cholas made significant military gains, capturing strategic regions of Sri Lanka and establishing control over important trade routes.

The Chola conquests had a profound impact on Sri Lankan society and governance. The Cholas introduced a new administrative system and appointed local Tamil governors to oversee their newly acquired territories. These governors, known as "mandalikas," exercised Chola authority and implemented their administrative policies, thereby solidifying Tamil influence in Sri Lanka.

The Tamil influence on Sri Lankan history extended beyond political governance. The Cholas brought with them their rich cultural heritage, including their language, literature, art, and architecture. Tamil traditions and practices permeated various aspects of Sri Lankan society, leaving a lasting impact on language, religious practices, and cultural expressions.

The Cholas' architectural and artistic influence is particularly evident in the magnificent temples they constructed throughout Sri Lanka. The architectural style and design of these Chola-influenced temples, characterized by intricate stone carvings, towering gopurams (gateway towers), and vibrant frescoes, reflect the artistic grandeur of the Chola dynasty.

One of the notable Chola-influenced temples in Sri Lanka is the Brihadisvara Kovil, located in the ancient city of Polonnaruwa. This temple stands as a testament to the architectural and artistic finesse of the Cholas, with its towering structure and elaborate carvings. The temple became a center for Tamil religious practices and continues to be revered by devotees.

The Chola influence on Sri Lankan literature and language is also significant. Tamil poetry and literary works found patronage in Sri Lanka during this period, contributing to the growth and development of Tamil literature on the island. The intertwining of Tamil and Sinhala cultural expressions resulted in a rich literary heritage that continues to be cherished today.

It is important to note that while the Chola conquests brought Tamil influence to Sri Lanka, they were not without challenges and resistance. The presence of Chola authority was met with opposition from local rulers and communities who sought to maintain their autonomy and cultural distinctiveness. This led to periods of conflict and shifting power dynamics on the island.

The Chola influence in Sri Lanka began to wane towards the latter part of the 11th century CE, as internal conflicts and external pressures weakened Chola rule. Eventually, the Cholas were forced to relinquish their control over Sri Lanka, and the island experienced a period of renewed autonomy under local rulers.

The legacy of the Chola conquests and Tamil influence on Sri Lankan history is a testament to the interconnectedness of South Indian and Sri Lankan cultures. It reminds us of the dynamic nature of historical developments, where the ebb and flow of empires and cultural exchanges shape the identity and heritage of nations.

Today, the Tamil influence in Sri Lanka can still be seen in various aspects of society, including language, religion, cuisine, and cultural practices. The contributions of the Cholas and their lasting impact on Sri Lankan history serve as a reminder of the enduring ties between the Tamil and Sinhala communities and the shared historical heritage they continue to embrace.

# The Golden Age of Sinhalese Literature: Poets and Scholars of the Classical Era

The classical era of Sri Lanka witnessed a flourishing of literature, intellectual pursuits, and artistic expression, often referred to as the Golden Age of Sinhalese Literature. This period, spanning from the 9th to the 14th centuries CE, produced a rich body of literary works, poems, and treatises that continue to be revered and cherished today. The poets and scholars of this era played a vital role in shaping the cultural and intellectual landscape of Sri Lanka.

During the Golden Age, Sri Lanka witnessed a resurgence of interest in scholarly pursuits, spurred by the patronage of kings and the establishment of monastic institutions dedicated to learning. Buddhist monasteries, or "pirivenas," became centers of intellectual activity, attracting scholars and nurturing a vibrant literary tradition.

Prominent among the poets and scholars of the classical era was King Parakramabahu the Great, known not only for his political acumen but also for his poetic prowess. His poetic compositions, such as the Kavisilumina, exemplify the lyrical beauty and sophistication of Sinhalese poetry. King Parakramabahu's patronage of the arts and literature set the stage for a vibrant literary scene that thrived under subsequent rulers.

One of the notable works of Sinhalese literature from this era is the Sandesa Kavya, a genre of poetry that emerged as a popular form of expression. These poems, often written in the form of letters or messages, showcased the skill and creativity of the poets in weaving intricate narratives and employing literary devices. The Sandesa Kavyas, such as the Kokila Sandesaya and the Gira Sandesaya, captured the imagination of the readers with their vivid descriptions, metaphors, and allegories.

The classical era also witnessed the composition of the Pansiya Panas Jataka, a collection of stories from the previous lives of the Buddha. These Jataka tales, written in verse form, not only entertained but also conveyed moral and ethical lessons to the readers. The Pansiya Panas Jataka, composed by a group of scholars known as the Atthakatha-Mahasangha, continues to be treasured as a literary masterpiece and a valuable source of Buddhist teachings.

Scholars and grammarians of the classical era played a crucial role in preserving and standardizing the Sinhalese language. Their meticulous study and analysis of grammar and syntax resulted in the compilation of treatises such as the Kaccayana, Amarakosha, and Saddharmaratnavaliya. These works served as reference texts, helping to refine and enrich the Sinhalese language and ensuring its longevity and continuity.

Among the notable scholars of the classical era, mention must be made of the renowned poet and scholar Alagiyavanna Mukaveti. He is credited with writing the Kausilumina, an epic poem that narrates the story of Prince Kausalya, drawing inspiration from the Ramayana. The Kausilumina is celebrated for its intricate verses, vivid imagery, and the depth of its philosophical reflections.

The classical era also witnessed the development of historical chronicles, known as "Mahavamsa" and

"Dipavamsa," which chronicled the lineage of the Sinhalese kings and provided valuable insights into the political, social, and religious landscape of the time. These chronicles were not only historical records but also served as literary works, reflecting the skill of the chroniclers in narrating historical events and legends with poetic flair.

It is important to note that the literary achievements of the classical era were not confined to royal courts and monastic institutions alone. There were numerous poets and scholars from diverse backgrounds who contributed to the rich tapestry of Sinhalese literature. They composed verses on various themes, including love, nature, religious devotion, and social commentary, reflecting the diverse range of interests and concerns of the time.

The legacy of the poets and scholars of the classical era endures in Sri Lankan literature and serves as a source of inspiration for contemporary writers and artists. Their contributions not only enriched the Sinhalese language but also fostered a sense of cultural identity and pride among the people.

In conclusion, the Golden Age of Sinhalese Literature during the classical era was marked by the remarkable achievements of poets and scholars who nurtured a vibrant literary tradition. Their works continue to resonate with readers, offering insights into the cultural, intellectual, and artistic aspirations of the time.

# Maritime Connections: Sri Lanka's Trade with the Ancient World

The geographical location of Sri Lanka, situated at a strategic point in the Indian Ocean, has endowed the island with a rich history of maritime connections and vibrant trade with the ancient world. From early civilizations to medieval empires, Sri Lanka's maritime trade routes played a crucial role in facilitating the exchange of goods, ideas, and cultural influences. This chapter explores the maritime connections of Sri Lanka, highlighting its significance as a hub of trade and commerce in antiquity.

The ancient maritime trade of Sri Lanka dates back thousands of years, with evidence of trading activities found in archaeological excavations and historical records. Sri Lanka's natural resources, such as gems, spices, ivory, pearls, and exotic woods, attracted merchants from distant lands who sought to acquire these coveted commodities.

One of the earliest recorded trade connections of Sri Lanka was with the ancient Egyptians. Egyptian artifacts, including pottery and beads, have been discovered in Sri Lankan archaeological sites, indicating a trade network that spanned the Indian Ocean. Sri Lanka's valuable resources, especially precious gems like sapphires and rubies, were highly sought after by the Egyptians for their decorative and symbolic purposes.

Sri Lanka's trade connections extended to other ancient civilizations as well. The island's proximity to the Roman Empire made it an important trading partner. Roman coins, ceramics, and glassware have been unearthed in Sri Lanka, pointing to a vibrant exchange of goods between the two regions. Sri Lanka's spices, particularly cinnamon, enjoyed great demand in the Roman market, further solidifying its position as a key player in the ancient trade network.

The island's trade connections also extended to the Chinese during the ancient period. Historical records and archaeological finds indicate that Sri Lanka was a crucial stop along the maritime Silk Road, facilitating trade between China and the rest of the Indian Ocean region. Chinese ceramics, silk, and other goods made their way to Sri Lanka, while Sri Lankan products, such as gems and spices, were highly valued by the Chinese.

Another significant maritime connection of Sri Lanka was with the Islamic world. The advent of Islam in the 7th century CE brought about increased trade and cultural interactions between Sri Lanka and the Arab merchants. Arab navigators, drawn to the island's strategic location and resources, established trade links and settlements along the coastal regions. The Arab influence on Sri Lanka's trade, language, and even the introduction of Islam itself left a lasting impact on the island's history.

The arrival of European powers in the Age of Exploration further transformed Sri Lanka's maritime connections. Portuguese, Dutch, and British traders vied for control over the island's resources and trade routes, leading to a complex colonial period in Sri Lankan history. The European powers sought to establish monopolies over key commodities, leading to significant changes in the island's trade dynamics.

The maritime connections of Sri Lanka were not limited to trade alone. They also facilitated cultural exchanges and the spread of ideas, religions, and languages. Buddhism, which originated in India, found its way to Sri Lanka through maritime routes, shaping the island's religious and cultural landscape. Sri Lanka's connection to the maritime Silk Road facilitated the spread of Buddhism to East Asia, exemplifying the far-reaching influence of the island's trade networks.

The importance of maritime connections to Sri Lanka's history cannot be overstated. The island's position as a crossroads of trade enabled the exchange of goods, technologies, knowledge, and cultural practices. It fostered a sense of interconnectedness and shaped the island's identity as a diverse and cosmopolitan society.

In conclusion, Sri Lanka's maritime connections with the ancient world were vital to its historical development. The island's strategic location, abundant resources, and vibrant trade routes established it as a hub of commercial and cultural interactions. Sri Lanka's maritime connections not only fueled economic prosperity but also facilitated the exchange of ideas, religions, and cultural influences that continue to resonate in the fabric of Sri Lankan society.

# Rise of the Kingdom of Kotte: Shifting Power Centers

The shifting dynamics of power and political control in Sri Lanka's history led to the rise and fall of various kingdoms. One such significant chapter is the emergence of the Kingdom of Kotte as a prominent power center during the medieval period. This chapter explores the rise of the Kingdom of Kotte, its political landscape, and its influence on Sri Lankan history.

The Kingdom of Kotte traces its origins to the late 14th century CE when Alagakkonara, a powerful minister of the Kingdom of Gampola, established his authority in the region. Alagakkonara's son, Vijayabahu, took control of the area around Kotte and established a separate kingdom, marking the foundation of the Kingdom of Kotte.

Under the reign of Vijayabahu, Kotte steadily grew in power and influence, eventually eclipsing the Kingdom of Gampola as the preeminent power in Sri Lanka. Vijayabahu adopted the title "Sri Parakramabahu" to legitimize his claim to power, evoking the memory of the great Sinhalese kings of the past.

The Kingdom of Kotte reached its zenith under the rule of King Parakramabahu VI, who ascended the throne in the mid-15th century CE. King Parakramabahu VI expanded the kingdom's territory through military conquests and established a well-organized administrative system. He transformed Kotte into a bustling capital, complete with impressive palaces, temples, and other architectural marvels.

One of the key features of the Kingdom of Kotte was its strategic location. Situated near the mouth of the Kelani River, Kotte offered easy access to maritime trade routes and facilitated economic prosperity. The kingdom became a center of trade and attracted merchants from diverse regions, contributing to its economic growth.

The rise of the Kingdom of Kotte also saw a significant shift in political and cultural dynamics. The capital city of Kotte became a melting pot of different ethnic and religious communities. While the Sinhalese remained the majority, there were also substantial populations of Tamils, Muslims, and other groups. This cultural diversity added to the vibrancy and cosmopolitan nature of the kingdom.

Kotte's political landscape was characterized by a complex web of alliances and rivalries. The Kingdom of Kotte had to contend with other powerful regional powers, such as the Kingdom of Jaffna in the north and the maritime powers of the time, including the Portuguese and the Kingdom of Kandy. These shifting alliances and conflicts shaped the course of Kotte's history and influenced its relationship with external powers.

The arrival of the Portuguese in the early 16th century CE had a significant impact on the Kingdom of Kotte. The Portuguese, driven by their desire for control over the lucrative spice trade, established their presence in Sri Lanka and gradually extended their authority over various coastal regions. The Kingdom of Kotte entered into a complex relationship with the Portuguese, often oscillating between cooperation and resistance.

Ultimately, the Kingdom of Kotte succumbed to Portuguese dominance. In 1565 CE, King Dharmapala, the last ruler of Kotte, ceded his kingdom to the Portuguese. This marked a turning point in Sri Lankan history, as Portuguese colonial rule came to prevail over the island.

The rise and fall of the Kingdom of Kotte represent a significant era in Sri Lanka's history. It symbolizes the shifting power centers and political dynamics that have shaped the island's trajectory. The legacy of the Kingdom of Kotte reminds us of the complexities of political alliances, territorial ambitions, and external influences that have played a role in shaping the destiny of Sri Lanka.

# European Encounters: Portuguese Exploration and Colonialism

The 15th century marked a turning point in world history with the dawn of European exploration and the age of colonialism. The Portuguese, driven by a desire for trade, wealth, and influence, embarked on daring voyages that brought them to distant lands, including Sri Lanka. This chapter explores the European encounters of the Portuguese in Sri Lanka, their explorations, and the impacts of their colonial presence.

The Portuguese, under the leadership of explorers such as Vasco da Gama and Pedro Álvares Cabral, sought to find new maritime routes to Asia, bypassing the monopolistic control of the established land routes. In 1498, Vasco da Gama successfully reached the shores of Calicut (present-day Kozhikode) in India, opening up a direct sea route between Europe and Asia.

The Portuguese, driven by their quest for spices and wealth, soon turned their attention to the Indian Ocean region, including Sri Lanka. They established a fortified presence in the coastal areas of Sri Lanka, particularly in Colombo, Galle, and Jaffna, as strategic bases for their maritime operations.

The arrival of the Portuguese in Sri Lanka had a profound impact on the island's political, economic, and social landscape. They brought with them superior naval technology and military prowess, which allowed them to assert their dominance over the local kingdoms. The

Portuguese established control over key coastal regions, disrupting existing power structures and trade networks.

One of the notable consequences of Portuguese presence in Sri Lanka was their influence on the island's religion. The Portuguese, driven by their fervent Catholic faith, sought to convert the local population to Christianity. They aggressively suppressed indigenous religious practices, often resorting to force and coercion. This led to tensions and conflicts with the local rulers and communities who sought to preserve their religious and cultural traditions.

The Portuguese also left a lasting impact on Sri Lanka's linguistic landscape. They introduced and promoted the use of the Portuguese language, resulting in a significant influence on the development of the local Creole language, known as Sri Lankan Portuguese Creole. This language, a blend of Portuguese, Tamil, and Sinhala, evolved as a means of communication between the Portuguese and the local population.

The Portuguese presence in Sri Lanka was not without resistance. Local kingdoms and regional powers, such as the Kingdom of Kandy and the Kingdom of Jaffna, fiercely resisted Portuguese encroachment on their territories. These kingdoms engaged in protracted conflicts with the Portuguese, seeking to preserve their independence and sovereignty.

The Portuguese influence on Sri Lanka's trade cannot be understated. They monopolized the spice trade and established control over key trading ports, including Colombo and Galle. The Portuguese exploited Sri Lanka's resources, particularly cinnamon, which was highly prized in European markets. This trade dominance brought wealth to the Portuguese but disrupted existing trade networks and adversely affected the local economy.

However, Portuguese colonial rule in Sri Lanka was not a long-lasting phenomenon. The Portuguese faced stiff resistance from regional powers and rival European powers. The Dutch, in particular, sought to challenge Portuguese dominance in the Indian Ocean and launched military campaigns to gain control over Sri Lanka's coastal regions.

By the 17th century, the Dutch succeeded in ousting the Portuguese and established their own colonial presence in Sri Lanka. The Dutch era marked a new chapter in Sri Lanka's colonial history, but it also led to further struggles for power and influence among European powers.

In conclusion, the European encounters of the Portuguese in Sri Lanka represented a pivotal moment in the island's history. The Portuguese exploration and colonial presence left a lasting impact on the political, religious, linguistic, and economic landscape of Sri Lanka. The consequences of their arrival shaped the trajectory of the island's subsequent colonial history and the complexities of its post-colonial identity.

# The Dutch Era: The VOC's Influence and the Changing Colonial Landscape

The Dutch Era in Sri Lanka's history marked a significant chapter in the island's colonial experience. The Dutch East India Company, known as the VOC (Vereenigde Oost-Indische Compagnie), arrived in Sri Lanka in the 17th century and established their presence, bringing about far-reaching changes in the political, economic, and social landscape. This chapter delves into the Dutch era, exploring the VOC's influence and the changing colonial landscape in Sri Lanka.

The arrival of the Dutch in Sri Lanka was driven by their desire to challenge Portuguese dominance in the Indian Ocean region. The VOC sought control over key maritime trade routes and access to valuable commodities, particularly spices. Sri Lanka's strategic location and resources made it a coveted territory for the Dutch, leading to protracted conflicts with the Portuguese and local kingdoms.

The Dutch gradually expanded their presence in Sri Lanka, capturing important coastal regions and establishing fortified settlements. They secured control over key ports, including Colombo, Galle, and Trincomalee, which became crucial trading centers for the VOC. The Dutch fortifications, such as the Galle Fort, stand as enduring symbols of their colonial influence.

One of the significant aspects of the Dutch era was their administrative and economic policies. The VOC implemented a system of indirect rule, working closely with local rulers and maintaining a dual administration known as the "Garrison System." This system allowed the Dutch to exercise control over trade and taxation while leaving the day-to-day governance to the local authorities.

The Dutch era brought about changes in land ownership and agricultural practices. The VOC introduced the "Land Rent System," which required local communities to pay rent for the use of land. This policy aimed to ensure a steady revenue stream for the Dutch and promoted the cultivation of cash crops, such as cinnamon, indigo, and coffee. This shift in agricultural practices had a lasting impact on Sri Lanka's economy and land distribution patterns.

Under Dutch rule, Christianity continued to be promoted, albeit with a different approach than the Portuguese. The Dutch adopted a more tolerant attitude towards the local religions, allowing religious freedom to a certain extent. They established Reformed Protestant churches, alongside Catholic and Anglican churches, catering to the needs of the diverse European and local Christian communities.

The Dutch era also witnessed the expansion of the Dutch influence beyond the coastal regions. They sought to extend their control over the Kingdom of Kandy, the last independent kingdom in Sri Lanka. However, their attempts to conquer Kandy proved unsuccessful, as the Kandyan Kingdom fiercely resisted Dutch encroachment, maintaining their autonomy and sovereignty.

Trade played a central role in the Dutch colonial enterprise in Sri Lanka. The VOC's monopolistic control over trade, especially the spice trade, brought immense wealth and prosperity to the Dutch. Sri Lanka's cinnamon, in particular, was highly valued in European markets, contributing to the Dutch economic dominance in the region. The VOC's trade connections spanned across continents, facilitating the exchange of goods, ideas, and cultural influences.

The Dutch era also witnessed the introduction of new technologies and cultural exchanges. The Dutch brought advanced agricultural techniques, such as irrigation systems and crop cultivation methods, which contributed to the development of Sri Lanka's agricultural sector. They also brought European-style architecture and town planning, leaving their architectural imprint in Sri Lankan cities and towns.

The changing colonial landscape in Sri Lanka during the Dutch era was not without challenges and resistance. Local uprisings, such as the rebellion led by King Rajasinghe II of Kandy, and the emergence of indigenous leaders like Keppetipola Disawe, demonstrated the enduring spirit of resistance against colonial rule. These uprisings highlighted the deep-rooted desire for independence and the preservation of local identity.

The Dutch presence in Sri Lanka gradually waned as their global influence declined. The British, emerging as a dominant colonial power in the Indian subcontinent, gained control over Sri Lanka through a series of diplomatic agreements and military campaigns. The British takeover in 1796 marked the end of the Dutch era and the beginning of a new chapter in Sri Lanka's colonial history.

In conclusion, the Dutch Era in Sri Lanka left a lasting imprint on the island's history. The VOC's influence brought about changes in governance, trade, agriculture, and cultural practices. The Dutch colonial legacy, while complex and contested, contributed to the shaping of Sri Lanka's colonial landscape and its subsequent path towards independence.

# The British Arrival: From Trading Post to Colonial Rule

The arrival of the British in Sri Lanka marked a significant chapter in the island's colonial history. What began as a desire for trade and maritime control eventually led to British colonial rule, profoundly shaping the political, economic, and social landscape of the island. This chapter delves into the British arrival in Sri Lanka, tracing the transformation from a trading post to full-fledged colonial rule.

The British interest in Sri Lanka was initially driven by its strategic location along the maritime trade routes to Asia. The British East India Company, following the footsteps of previous European powers, sought to establish a foothold in the Indian Ocean region. In 1796, the British took control of the coastal areas, including Colombo, Galle, and Trincomalee, from the Dutch, marking the beginning of their presence in Sri Lanka.

Initially, the British viewed Sri Lanka primarily as a trading post, aiming to exploit the island's resources and establish control over its trade networks. Under the British East India Company's administration, the island experienced relative stability and a continuation of existing administrative structures. The British initially upheld the Dutch Garrison System, allowing local authorities to maintain control over internal affairs while the British oversaw external trade and defense.

However, the trajectory of British presence in Sri Lanka shifted with the abolition of the Dutch East India Company in 1798. The British government assumed direct control over the administration of the island, transforming Sri Lanka into a Crown colony. This change marked the beginning of British colonial rule, leading to profound changes in governance, land ownership, and cultural practices.

Under British colonial rule, the island was renamed Ceylon, a name that persisted until Sri Lanka gained independence in 1948. The British administration introduced new systems of governance, including a centralized administrative structure, a formal legal system, and British-style education. These changes aimed to assert British control and facilitate the smooth functioning of colonial rule.

The British influence extended beyond governance. The introduction of plantation agriculture became a defining feature of the colonial economy. The British, driven by profit and the demand for cash crops in Europe, established vast tea, coffee, rubber, and coconut plantations. The plantation economy relied heavily on labor, leading to the importation of Tamil and Sinhalese workers from South India, resulting in demographic shifts and cultural influences.

The British colonial rule also brought about changes in land ownership and land tenure systems. The British implemented various land policies, including the Waste Land Ordinance and the Crown Land Encroachment Ordinance, which allowed for the acquisition of land for plantation agriculture. These policies resulted in the dispossession of indigenous communities from their ancestral lands and the consolidation of land ownership in the hands of the British and a small elite.

The British colonial period witnessed the spread of Western education and cultural influences. Missionary schools were established, introducing English education and Christian values. The English language gained prominence and became a symbol of prestige and upward mobility. The introduction of modern infrastructure, such as railways, roads, and ports, transformed the island's connectivity and facilitated trade and commerce.

The impact of British colonial rule was not uniform across all communities. The Tamil and Muslim communities, in particular, were affected by cultural and economic changes. The British favored Tamils in administrative positions, contributing to a sense of inequality among the Sinhalese majority. These dynamics would later shape political movements and tensions in the post-independence era.

The British presence in Sri Lanka was not without resistance. Indigenous uprisings, such as the 1817-1818 Uva Rebellion, demonstrated the discontent and opposition to British rule. The resistance movements were met with harsh repression, leading to loss of life and significant social upheaval. These uprisings reflect the deep-rooted desire for independence and the preservation of local traditions and identity.

The British colonial era in Sri Lanka gradually paved the way for a nascent nationalist movement. The introduction of Western education, exposure to democratic ideals, and economic disparities fueled demands for self-governance and independence. Political organizations, such as the Ceylon National Congress and later the Sri Lankan independence movement, emerged, advocating for increased autonomy and eventual freedom from British rule.

In 1948, Sri Lanka gained independence from the British Empire, marking the end of nearly 150 years of British colonial rule. The legacies of British colonialism continue to shape the social, economic, and political dynamics of the island, serving as a reminder of the complexities and challenges faced in the post-colonial era.

In conclusion, the British arrival in Sri Lanka transformed the island from a trading post to a full-fledged colony. British colonial rule left a lasting impact on the governance, economy, and cultural fabric of Sri Lanka. The dynamics of power, resistance, and eventual independence shaped the path towards nationhood and the challenges faced by the newly independent country.

# Coffee, Tea, and Rubber: Plantation Economy and British Rule

The period of British colonial rule in Sri Lanka witnessed the emergence and expansion of a plantation economy centered around the cultivation and export of cash crops, particularly coffee, tea, and rubber. This chapter explores the development of the plantation economy under British rule, its impact on the island's economy and society, and the enduring legacy of this economic model.

The British, driven by their quest for profit and the demand for commodities in Europe, introduced the plantation system to Sri Lanka. The island's favorable climate and fertile land were conducive to the cultivation of cash crops. The British established large-scale plantations, transforming vast stretches of land into productive estates.

Coffee was the first major cash crop introduced by the British. The coffee plantations, particularly in the central highlands, thrived during the early to mid-19th century. The export of coffee brought considerable wealth and economic growth to the colony, attracting both British and local investors. The plantation sector became a key contributor to the island's economy.

However, the prosperity of the coffee industry was short-lived. In the 1860s, a devastating coffee leaf disease, known as coffee rust, struck the plantations, decimating the coffee crops. The loss of coffee plantations led to a significant economic setback and prompted a search for alternative crops.

Tea emerged as a viable alternative to coffee in the late 19th century. The British, with their expertise in tea cultivation from India, introduced tea plantations in the central highlands of Sri Lanka. The cool climate and rich soil proved ideal for tea cultivation, and the industry quickly gained momentum. Sri Lanka, then known as Ceylon, became renowned for its high-quality teas and established itself as a leading global tea exporter.

The tea industry brought significant economic benefits to Sri Lanka. Plantations expanded rapidly, covering vast areas of the central highlands. Tea estates employed a large workforce, including Tamils from South India who were brought in as laborers. The tea trade stimulated infrastructure development, including railways, roads, and processing factories, further contributing to economic growth.

The plantation economy also witnessed the rise of the rubber industry. The British introduced rubber cultivation in Sri Lanka in the late 19th century, primarily in the low-lying areas of the island. Rubber plantations expanded rapidly, driven by the growing global demand for rubber products. Sri Lanka became a major rubber producer, exporting latex to international markets.

The plantation economy had a profound impact on the social fabric of Sri Lanka. The large-scale plantations relied heavily on labor, leading to the importation of indentured workers from South India. These workers, predominantly Tamils, formed the backbone of the plantation workforce. Their arrival significantly influenced demographic patterns, cultural exchanges, and the emergence of distinct communities within the island.

The plantation sector was characterized by a hierarchical system. British planters and administrators held positions of power, while the local workforce, comprising laborers and estate workers, faced challenging working conditions and low wages. This division created economic disparities and social tensions that persist to some extent to this day.

The plantation economy also had implications for land ownership. The British implemented land policies, such as the Waste Land Ordinance, that facilitated the acquisition of land for plantations. Indigenous communities, who traditionally had a connection to the land, faced displacement and dispossession, resulting in the consolidation of land ownership in the hands of the British and a small elite.

The plantation economy under British rule had a transformative effect on Sri Lanka's economy, infrastructure, and cultural landscape. It played a pivotal role in shaping the island's export-oriented economy and establishing its reputation as a global supplier of agricultural commodities. The legacy of the plantation economy continues to impact Sri Lanka's economy and society, with tea and rubber remaining important industries to this day.

In conclusion, the plantation economy of coffee, tea, and rubber under British rule reshaped Sri Lanka's economic and social landscape. The introduction of cash crops brought economic growth, infrastructure development, and demographic shifts. However, it also entailed challenges such as labor exploitation, land dispossession, and socio-economic disparities that have influenced the country's history and development.

# Sri Lankan Independence Movement: Awakening National Consciousness

The early 20th century witnessed the awakening of national consciousness and the emergence of the Sri Lankan independence movement. This chapter explores the journey towards independence, highlighting the key events, leaders, and movements that shaped Sri Lanka's path to self-governance.

The seeds of the independence movement were sown during the latter part of British colonial rule. The introduction of Western education, exposure to democratic ideals, and economic disparities fueled demands for self-governance and national identity. Sri Lankans from various communities began to question the legitimacy of foreign rule and sought avenues for political participation.

The Ceylon National Congress, founded in 1919, became a significant platform for Sri Lankan nationalists to voice their aspirations for independence. Led by prominent figures such as D.S. Senanayake, F.R. Senanayake, and E.W. Perera, the Ceylon National Congress advocated for increased autonomy and eventual self-rule.

The movement for independence gained momentum in the 1920s and 1930s, driven by a series of key events and developments. One such milestone was the Donoughmore Commission of 1927, which recommended constitutional reforms and limited representative government. The introduction of these reforms, although partial, marked a significant step towards political empowerment for the Sri Lankan people.

The independence movement was characterized by the participation of individuals from diverse communities, transcending ethnic, religious, and social barriers. Tamil leaders such as Sir Ponnambalam Arunachalam and G.G. Ponnambalam played crucial roles in advocating for Tamil rights within the broader framework of the independence movement. They emphasized the need for communal harmony and equal representation.

The political landscape of Sri Lanka during the independence movement was marked by various political parties and ideologies. The All Ceylon Tamil Congress, led by G.G. Ponnambalam, championed Tamil rights, while the Lanka Sama Samaja Party and the Communist Party of Sri Lanka espoused socialist and leftist principles. These parties, along with the Ceylon National Congress, galvanized public support for the cause of independence.

The struggle for independence was not limited to political parties alone. Civil society organizations, trade unions, and student movements also played pivotal roles in shaping the national consciousness and mobilizing public support. Organizations such as the Ceylon National Association for the Advancement of Women, the Ceylon Labour Union, and the Jaffna Youth Congress contributed to the broader movement for independence.

The Second World War proved to be a turning point in Sri Lanka's journey towards independence. The war created fissures in the colonial administration, and the British were compelled to make concessions to nationalist demands. The Soulbury Commission of 1944 led to the granting of further constitutional reforms and increased self-governance, paving the way for the eventual transfer of power.

The post-war period witnessed intensified efforts by Sri Lankan nationalists to accelerate the pace of independence. In 1947, the British government announced plans for the granting of independence to Sri Lanka. On February 4, 1948, Sri Lanka, then known as Ceylon, achieved independence from British colonial rule, marking a historic milestone in the island's history.

The transition to independence was not without challenges. The Sri Lankan independence movement faced complex issues of communal harmony, language rights, and representation. The language policy debates between Sinhala and Tamil communities, for instance, gave rise to tensions that would later shape the socio-political landscape of the country.

In conclusion, the Sri Lankan independence movement represents a significant chapter in the island's history. The awakening of national consciousness, the emergence of political parties and organizations, and the tireless efforts of leaders and activists paved the way for Sri Lanka's journey towards self-governance. The achievements and challenges of the independence movement continue to shape the country's path as an independent nation.

# Post-Independence Politics: From Dominion Status to Republic

The post-independence era in Sri Lanka was marked by significant political developments, as the country navigated its path towards self-governance and addressed various challenges associated with nation-building. This chapter explores the political landscape of Sri Lanka from the attainment of dominion status to the transition into a republic.

Following independence in 1948, Sri Lanka became a dominion within the British Commonwealth. Under the leadership of D.S. Senanayake, who served as the first Prime Minister, the country embarked on a journey to establish a stable political system and address socio-economic disparities. The dominant political party during this period was the United National Party (UNP).

The early years of independence were focused on building the foundations of a new nation. Sri Lanka's political leaders faced the challenges of consolidating a diverse society, reconciling ethnic and religious differences, and promoting national unity. Efforts were made to strengthen democratic institutions, promote economic development, and enhance social welfare.

One of the key achievements during this period was the passage of the Soulbury Constitution in 1947, which provided a framework for self-governance and laid the groundwork for democratic governance. The constitution established a parliamentary system with a bicameral legislature and guaranteed certain fundamental rights and freedoms to the citizens of Sri Lanka.

The post-independence period also witnessed the rise of political movements that sought to address the concerns and aspirations of different communities. The Tamil Arasu Kachchi (Federal Party), led by S.J.V. Chelvanayakam, advocated for Tamil rights and regional autonomy within a federal structure. This marked the emergence of ethno-political dynamics that would later shape the country's political landscape.

In 1972, Sri Lanka underwent a significant constitutional transformation, transitioning from a dominion to a republic. The new constitution, known as the First Republican Constitution, severed the remaining constitutional ties with the British monarchy and established Sri Lanka as an independent republic. This constitutional change was led by the Sri Lanka Freedom Party (SLFP) under the leadership of Sirimavo Bandaranaike.

The transition to a republic also brought about changes in the political structure and governance of the country. The executive presidency was introduced, concentrating significant powers in the hands of the president. This shift in power dynamics would later have a profound impact on Sri Lanka's political landscape and the dynamics between different branches of government.

Post-independence politics in Sri Lanka were marked by the emergence of multiple political parties and the rise of electoral competition. The two main political parties, the UNP and the SLFP, dominated the political scene and engaged in intense political rivalries. The political landscape was characterized by alternating periods of power between these two parties, with subsequent governments pursuing their own political agendas.

The post-independence period also witnessed the emergence of socialist and Marxist political movements, such as the Lanka Sama Samaja Party (LSSP) and the Communist Party of Sri Lanka. These parties advocated for social justice, workers' rights, and greater equality. Their influence had a significant impact on shaping the socio-political discourse in the country.

Sri Lanka's post-independence political journey was not without challenges. The country faced complex issues related to ethnic and religious tensions, language policy, regional disparities, and the management of resources. These challenges often manifested in political struggles, social unrest, and periodic conflicts, underscoring the complexities of governance in a multi-ethnic and multi-religious society.

In conclusion, the post-independence era in Sri Lanka witnessed a dynamic political landscape as the country transitioned from dominion status to a republic. The political developments during this period played a crucial role in shaping the nation's political institutions, identity, and the challenges it would face in the years to come.

# Ethnic Tensions and Communal Strife: The Roots of Conflict

Sri Lanka's history has been marked by ethnic tensions and communal strife, rooted in complex social, cultural, and political factors. This chapter delves into the origins and dynamics of ethnic tensions in Sri Lanka, exploring the underlying causes that have contributed to communal conflicts throughout the country's history.

Ethnic tensions in Sri Lanka can be traced back to the colonial era when British policies and administrative practices created divisions among communities. The British favored certain communities, particularly the Tamils, in terms of education, employment opportunities, and administrative positions. This differential treatment sowed the seeds of discontent and laid the groundwork for future ethnic tensions.

The issue of language has been a significant point of contention in Sri Lanka's history. The promotion of English as the language of governance and education during colonial rule marginalized the native languages, Sinhala and Tamil. This language policy disparity later fueled ethnic divisions, with language becoming a symbol of identity and representation.

The post-independence period witnessed the crystallization of ethnic identities and the emergence of ethno-nationalist politics. The Sinhalese majority, seeking to assert their cultural and political dominance, advocated for policies that favored Sinhala language, Buddhism, and the protection of Sinhalese interests. Concurrently, Tamil leaders began championing the rights and aspirations of the Tamil community, advocating for linguistic and regional autonomy.

The passage of the Official Language Act in 1956, which made Sinhala the sole official language of Sri Lanka, and subsequent policies that marginalized the Tamil language, further exacerbated ethnic tensions. These policies were seen as discriminatory by the Tamil community, leading to widespread protests and a sense of alienation.

Communal conflicts escalated in the 1970s and 1980s, leading to the outbreak of armed conflicts between the government and Tamil militant groups. The Liberation Tigers of Tamil Eelam (LTTE) emerged as the most prominent militant group, advocating for an independent Tamil state in the north and east of the country. The prolonged conflict resulted in a significant loss of life, displacement of populations, and a deepening of ethnic divisions.

The underlying causes of ethnic tensions in Sri Lanka are multi-faceted. They encompass issues of political power-sharing, language rights, economic disparities, land ownership, and the preservation of cultural identities. These factors, combined with historical grievances and the legacy of colonialism, have contributed to the deep-rooted nature of communal strife in Sri Lanka.

It is essential to recognize that ethnic tensions are not unique to Sri Lanka and are prevalent in many multi-ethnic societies undergoing socio-political transformations. The complex nature of these tensions requires comprehensive efforts towards reconciliation, understanding, and dialogue to foster a peaceful coexistence among different communities.

In recent years, Sri Lanka has taken steps towards reconciliation and peace-building. The end of the armed conflict in 2009 marked a significant milestone, creating an opportunity for healing and addressing the root causes of ethnic tensions. The establishment of mechanisms such as the Office for National Unity and Reconciliation and the Office on Missing Persons demonstrates the commitment to addressing past injustices and fostering national harmony.

Moving forward, it is crucial for Sri Lanka to address the underlying causes of ethnic tensions, promote inclusivity, and create an environment where all communities can coexist with dignity and equality. This requires efforts to bridge divides, promote cultural understanding, and ensure meaningful representation of all communities in the political and governance structures of the country.

In conclusion, ethnic tensions and communal strife in Sri Lanka have deep historical and socio-political roots. Understanding the complexities of these tensions is essential in working towards reconciliation, social cohesion, and a peaceful future for all communities in Sri Lanka.

# Cultural Revival: The Revitalization of Traditional Arts and Crafts

In the face of the challenges and complexities of Sri Lanka's history, there has been a remarkable resurgence and revival of traditional arts and crafts, representing a significant cultural revival. This chapter explores the revitalization of Sri Lanka's traditional arts and crafts, highlighting the efforts to preserve, promote, and celebrate the rich cultural heritage of the island.

Sri Lanka's traditional arts and crafts have a long and storied history, deeply rooted in the diverse communities that call the island home. These artistic expressions encompass a wide range of disciplines, including visual arts, performing arts, handloom weaving, wood carving, metalwork, pottery, and traditional dance forms.

The cultural revival movement gained momentum in the latter half of the 20th century, as Sri Lankans sought to reconnect with their roots and preserve the distinctive artistic traditions of their respective communities. This resurgence was driven by a growing recognition of the importance of cultural heritage, the desire to promote national identity, and the efforts of artists, artisans, and cultural enthusiasts.

One significant aspect of the cultural revival has been the establishment of cultural institutions and organizations dedicated to preserving and promoting traditional arts and crafts. Institutions such as the National Crafts Council, the National Arts Council, and the Department of Cultural Affairs have played pivotal roles in providing support, resources, and platforms for artists and artisans to showcase their work.

Efforts to revitalize traditional arts and crafts have encompassed various initiatives, including research, documentation, skills training, and the promotion of traditional craftsmanship. These endeavors have helped preserve traditional knowledge, techniques, and aesthetics, ensuring their transmission to future generations.

The revival of traditional arts and crafts has also been facilitated by the recognition and support from the government and non-governmental organizations. Programs and initiatives have been launched to provide financial assistance, training opportunities, and market access to artisans, enabling them to sustain their livelihoods and contribute to the preservation of cultural heritage.

Traditional festivals and cultural events have played a crucial role in promoting and celebrating Sri Lanka's traditional arts and crafts. Festivals like the Kandy Esala Perahera, the Navaratri festival, and the Vesak festival showcase traditional dance, music, and craftsmanship, attracting both local and international audiences.

In recent years, there has been a renewed appreciation for Sri Lanka's traditional arts and crafts in the global arena. Handloom textiles, wood carvings, and intricate metalwork have gained recognition for their craftsmanship and cultural significance. This recognition has opened up new opportunities for artisans to showcase their work internationally, contributing to the economic empowerment of communities involved in these traditional crafts.

The cultural revival movement has not only preserved and promoted traditional arts and crafts but has also fostered a sense of pride, identity, and community cohesion. Traditional art forms and craftsmanship have become sources of inspiration and cultural expression, reflecting the diversity and richness of Sri Lanka's cultural heritage.

Moreover, the cultural revival has had a positive impact on tourism, attracting visitors who are interested in experiencing the authentic cultural traditions of Sri Lanka. Traditional arts and crafts have become an integral part of the tourism industry, with craft villages, art galleries, and cultural centers offering immersive experiences for tourists.

In conclusion, the cultural revival in Sri Lanka has breathed new life into traditional arts and crafts, celebrating and preserving the island's cultural heritage. The efforts to revitalize these artistic traditions have not only contributed to the economic empowerment of artisans but also fostered a sense of identity and pride among the Sri Lankan people.

# The Sri Lankan Civil War: Causes, Conflicts, and Consequences

The Sri Lankan Civil War, spanning from 1983 to 2009, was a protracted and devastating conflict that deeply impacted the nation and its people. This chapter delves into the causes, conflicts, and consequences of the civil war, aiming to provide a comprehensive understanding of the complex dynamics surrounding this tragic period in Sri Lanka's history.

The origins of the civil war can be traced back to deep-seated ethnic tensions and grievances that had been simmering for decades. These tensions were rooted in issues of identity, language rights, political power-sharing, and economic disparities between the majority Sinhalese community and the Tamil minority.

The demand for a separate Tamil state, known as Tamil Eelam, was a central rallying cry of Tamil nationalist groups. They argued that the Tamil community had been marginalized and discriminated against by successive governments, leading to a sense of alienation and the desire for self-determination.

The conflict escalated in the early 1980s when violent clashes erupted between the Liberation Tigers of Tamil Eelam (LTTE), a militant group fighting for Tamil self-rule, and the Sri Lankan government. The LTTE, led by Velupillai Prabhakaran, employed guerrilla tactics and suicide bombings, while the government responded with military force.

The civil war witnessed a cycle of violence, with both sides engaged in acts of terrorism, human rights abuses, and war crimes. The LTTE carried out high-profile attacks, including the assassination of political figures and suicide bombings targeting civilians. The Sri Lankan armed forces conducted military operations, leading to civilian casualties and widespread displacement.

The conflict had a profound impact on the civilian population, particularly in the Tamil-majority areas in the north and east of the country. Communities were uprooted from their homes, with thousands of people displaced and forced to live in refugee camps or seek shelter in other parts of the country. Humanitarian conditions deteriorated, and basic necessities such as food, water, and healthcare became scarce.

Efforts to negotiate a peaceful resolution to the conflict were made at various times. The government entered into ceasefire agreements with the LTTE in the past, but these agreements ultimately broke down, leading to a resumption of hostilities. International actors, including neighboring countries and the international community, were involved in peace initiatives, but achieving a lasting solution proved elusive.

The turning point in the civil war came in 2009 when the Sri Lankan military launched a major offensive against the LTTE-held territory in the north. The military campaign, known as Operation Definite Victory, resulted in the defeat of the LTTE and the death of its leader, Velupillai Prabhakaran. The government declared an end to the civil war, marking a significant milestone in Sri Lanka's history.

The consequences of the civil war were profound and far-reaching. The loss of life, destruction of infrastructure, displacement of communities, and the deep scars left on the social fabric of the nation cannot be overstated. The conflict also strained ethnic relations and widened the divide between communities, leading to a long and challenging road towards reconciliation and healing.

In the post-war period, Sri Lanka has focused on rebuilding and reconciliation. Efforts have been made to address the grievances of affected communities, provide assistance to war-affected individuals, and promote national unity. Initiatives such as the Lessons Learned and Reconciliation Commission and the Office of Missing Persons have been established to address human rights violations and facilitate truth-seeking and justice.

It is essential to approach the topic of the Sri Lankan Civil War with sensitivity, recognizing the pain and trauma experienced by all communities involved. Moving forward, it is crucial to continue working towards lasting peace, reconciliation, and socio-economic development for all Sri Lankans, irrespective of their ethnic or religious backgrounds.

In conclusion, the Sri Lankan Civil War was a complex and tragic chapter in the nation's history, driven by deep-rooted ethnic tensions and grievances. The conflict resulted in immense human suffering and lasting consequences. The path towards reconciliation and healing requires a comprehensive and inclusive approach that addresses the root causes of the conflict and fosters a spirit of understanding and unity among all communities.

# Wildlife Wonderland: Biodiversity and Conservation Efforts

Sri Lanka is known for its remarkable biodiversity and rich wildlife, making it a true wildlife wonderland. This chapter explores the country's diverse ecosystems, unique flora and fauna, and the ongoing efforts to conserve and protect its natural treasures.

Sri Lanka's geographical location and varied climate contribute to its incredible biodiversity. The island is home to a wide range of habitats, including tropical rainforests, dry scrublands, wetlands, highland forests, and coastal ecosystems. Each of these ecosystems supports a distinct array of plant and animal species, creating a tapestry of biodiversity.

The island's wildlife is incredibly diverse, with a remarkable number of endemic species found nowhere else on earth. Sri Lanka boasts a high level of endemism, which means many plants and animals are unique to the island. This includes species such as the Sri Lankan leopard, the Sri Lankan elephant, the purple-faced langur, the toque macaque, and a variety of colorful bird species like the Sri Lanka junglefowl and the Sri Lanka blue magpie.

One of Sri Lanka's most iconic wildlife destinations is its national parks and protected areas. These protected areas encompass diverse ecosystems and provide crucial habitats for a wide range of wildlife. Yala National Park, Wilpattu National Park, Udawalawe National Park, and Sinharaja Forest Reserve are among the renowned reserves where visitors can witness the country's incredible wildlife up close.

The Sri Lankan elephant holds a special place in the country's wildlife heritage. The island is home to a significant population of these majestic creatures, and several national parks, such as Udawalawe and Minneriya, are famous for their elephant gatherings. Efforts are underway to protect and conserve elephant populations, including the establishment of elephant corridors and implementing conservation strategies to mitigate human-elephant conflicts.

Birdwatching enthusiasts are in for a treat in Sri Lanka, as the country offers exceptional avian diversity. Over 400 bird species have been recorded, ranging from colorful resident birds to migratory species. The Kumana National Park, Bundala National Park, and Sinharaja Forest Reserve are popular birding hotspots, attracting both local and international birdwatchers.

Marine life in Sri Lanka is equally captivating, with vibrant coral reefs, diverse fish species, and majestic marine mammals. The surrounding waters are frequented by dolphins, whales, and sea turtles. The waters off the southern coast, particularly Mirissa and Kalpitiya, are renowned for whale and dolphin watching, providing visitors with unforgettable experiences.

Conservation efforts play a vital role in safeguarding Sri Lanka's biodiversity and natural habitats. The Department of Wildlife Conservation, along with various non-governmental organizations and international partners, actively engage in conservation initiatives across the country. These efforts encompass habitat restoration, wildlife monitoring, community engagement, and awareness campaigns to promote sustainable practices and reduce human-wildlife conflicts.

The Sri Lankan government has taken steps to protect its natural treasures through the establishment of national parks, wildlife reserves, and marine protected areas. These protected areas provide a safe haven for wildlife and help preserve critical ecosystems. Strict regulations and anti-poaching measures are in place to combat illegal activities that threaten biodiversity. Community involvement in conservation is essential for long-term success. Local communities living near wildlife habitats actively participate in conservation initiatives, recognizing the importance of preserving their natural heritage. Community-based eco-tourism initiatives provide economic opportunities while raising awareness about the significance of protecting wildlife and habitats.

Sri Lanka's commitment to conservation extends beyond its borders. The country is a signatory to international agreements and conventions aimed at protecting endangered species and their habitats. Collaboration with global conservation organizations and participation in conservation research and monitoring programs further enhance conservation efforts.

In conclusion, Sri Lanka's wildlife is a testament to its remarkable biodiversity and serves as a wildlife wonderland. The country's diverse ecosystems, endemic species, and stunning landscapes make it a haven for nature lovers. Ongoing conservation efforts, backed by government initiatives and community involvement, ensure the protection of Sri Lanka's natural treasures for future generations to appreciate and enjoy.

# Ancient Irrigation Systems: The Ingenious Hydraulic Heritage

Sri Lanka's ancient irrigation systems stand as a testament to the island's rich hydraulic heritage and the ingenuity of its ancient engineers. This chapter explores the remarkable irrigation systems developed by ancient Sri Lankans, showcasing their advanced engineering skills, mastery of water management, and the lasting impact these systems have had on the country's agriculture and society.

Dating back thousands of years, Sri Lanka's ancient irrigation systems played a vital role in supporting agricultural activities and sustaining communities. These systems consisted of a network of interconnected tanks, reservoirs, canals, and channels, designed to harness and distribute water efficiently across different regions.

One of the most remarkable ancient irrigation systems in Sri Lanka is the "Tank Cascade System." This system involved creating a series of interconnected tanks at different elevations, allowing water to flow from higher to lower tanks through gravity. The tanks were strategically placed to collect and store rainwater during the wet season and release it gradually during the dry season for agricultural purposes.

The construction of these tanks required meticulous planning, engineering expertise, and extensive manual labor. Ancient Sri Lankan engineers employed various techniques to ensure the durability and efficiency of the tanks. The bunds or embankments surrounding the tanks were constructed with layers of compacted earth, fortified with stone or clay, and sometimes reinforced with tree trunks. These techniques helped prevent seepage and maintain the water levels in the tanks.

An integral part of the ancient irrigation systems was the construction of canals and channels to distribute water from the tanks to agricultural fields. These canals were designed with careful precision, taking into consideration the natural contours of the land and the topography of the region. The irrigation water was channeled through an intricate network of canals, ensuring a reliable supply of water to farmers throughout the year.

The ancient Sri Lankan irrigation systems also incorporated sophisticated water management techniques. A system of sluices, weirs, and gates was used to control the flow of water and regulate the distribution to different fields. These mechanisms allowed for optimal utilization of water resources and facilitated equitable distribution among farmers.

The impact of these ancient irrigation systems on agriculture and society cannot be overstated. The availability of water throughout the year enabled farmers to cultivate multiple crops and boost agricultural productivity. The surplus food production not only sustained local communities but also contributed to the prosperity of ancient Sri Lankan kingdoms.

The success of these ancient irrigation systems fostered a sense of community and collective responsibility among farmers. Water allocation and maintenance of the irrigation infrastructure were managed through a system of communal participation known as "Gam Sabhas." These community-based organizations played a crucial role in resolving disputes, ensuring fair distribution of water resources, and maintaining the irrigation infrastructure.

The ancient irrigation systems also had wider implications beyond agriculture. The abundance of water facilitated the growth of civilization, leading to the development of urban centers and the emergence of sophisticated societies. The availability of water for irrigation purposes enabled the establishment of settlements and the growth of trade and commerce.

The legacy of Sri Lanka's ancient irrigation systems can still be observed today. Many of these ancient tanks and canals continue to serve their original purpose, providing water for agriculture and supporting rural livelihoods. Some have even been recognized as UNESCO World Heritage Sites, such as the "Ancient City of Polonnaruwa," which showcases the intricate hydraulic infrastructure of the time.

In conclusion, Sri Lanka's ancient irrigation systems represent a remarkable feat of engineering and water management. The ingenuity and technical expertise of ancient Sri Lankan engineers have left a lasting legacy, shaping the country's agricultural practices, societal structure, and cultural heritage. These ancient irrigation systems stand as a testament to the wisdom of the past and serve as a source of inspiration for sustainable water management in the present and future.

# The Legacy of Ancient Architecture: Stupas, Temples, and Palaces

Sri Lanka's ancient architecture holds a rich legacy that showcases the country's cultural and artistic heritage. From majestic stupas to intricate temples and grand palaces, this chapter explores the diverse architectural wonders of ancient Sri Lanka, highlighting their significance, unique features, and enduring influence on the country's cultural landscape.

One of the most iconic architectural forms in Sri Lanka is the stupa, also known as a dagoba or cetiya. Stupas are sacred Buddhist structures designed to enshrine relics of the Buddha or other revered individuals. These domed structures symbolize the enlightened mind and serve as focal points for worship and meditation.

The Ruwanwelisaya stupa in Anuradhapura is a prime example of ancient stupa architecture. Standing at an impressive height, it is one of the tallest stupas in Sri Lanka and has withstood the test of time. The stupa's design features a large hemispherical dome, adorned with intricate carvings, statues, and a pinnacle known as a harmika. The surrounding ambulatory and circumambulatory path allow devotees to engage in ritualistic practices while circumambulating the stupa.

Temples are another prominent feature of ancient Sri Lankan architecture. These structures serve as places of worship and spiritual solace for adherents of Buddhism, Hinduism, and other religions. The architectural styles of ancient temples in Sri Lanka showcase a fusion of indigenous elements with influences from South India and Southeast Asia.

The Temple of the Tooth Relic (Sri Dalada Maligawa) in Kandy holds immense religious and cultural significance. It houses the sacred tooth relic of the Buddha and is considered one of the holiest sites in Sri Lanka. The temple's architecture exhibits Kandyan style, characterized by intricate woodwork, gabled roofs, and elaborate carvings depicting mythological and religious motifs.

The rock-cut cave temples of Dambulla are another remarkable example of ancient Sri Lankan architecture. The Dambulla Cave Temple complex, consisting of five caves adorned with intricate frescoes and hundreds of statues, showcases the fusion of religious and artistic expression. The caves serve as sanctuaries for Buddhist monks and are a testament to the country's ancient rock-cut architecture.

Ancient Sri Lanka was also home to magnificent palace complexes that served as centers of power and governance. The Sigiriya Rock Fortress is an extraordinary example of ancient palace architecture and engineering. Perched atop a massive rock formation, the palace complex features intricate water gardens, frescoes, and defensive structures. Sigiriya is a UNESCO World Heritage Site and a testament to the architectural brilliance of ancient Sri Lanka.

The architecture of ancient Sri Lanka was not solely confined to religious and palace structures. Ancient cities such as Anuradhapura and Polonnaruwa boasted a range of civic buildings, including royal audience halls, council chambers, and bathing ponds. These structures exhibited a sophisticated understanding of engineering, aesthetics, and urban planning.

The enduring influence of ancient Sri Lankan architecture can be seen in contemporary architectural practices and the preservation of cultural heritage. Traditional architectural elements and motifs continue to inspire modern designers, who incorporate them into contemporary structures. Restoration and conservation efforts are also undertaken to preserve and protect ancient architectural marvels, ensuring their legacy for future generations.

The architectural legacy of ancient Sri Lanka reflects the creativity, ingenuity, and spiritual devotion of its people. The structures embody a harmonious integration of form and function, blending aesthetics with religious and cultural symbolism. They stand as tangible evidence of Sri Lanka's rich architectural heritage and continue to inspire awe and admiration for their timeless beauty.

In conclusion, the legacy of ancient architecture in Sri Lanka is a testament to the country's artistic prowess, cultural diversity, and spiritual traditions. Stupas, temples, and palaces stand as enduring symbols of the country's rich heritage and continue to captivate visitors with their architectural splendor and historical significance.

# Folklore and Legends: Myths and Tales of Sri Lanka

Sri Lanka's rich cultural tapestry is interwoven with a vibrant collection of folklore and legends that have been passed down through generations. These myths and tales form an integral part of the country's oral tradition, offering insights into the beliefs, values, and imagination of the Sri Lankan people. This chapter delves into the diverse folklore and legends of Sri Lanka, exploring their origins, themes, and enduring significance.

One prominent figure in Sri Lankan folklore is the legendary King Ravana. According to the Hindu epic Ramayana, Ravana was a powerful king of Lanka (now Sri Lanka) and a central character in the tale of Prince Rama's quest to rescue his wife, Sita. The story of Ravana, his ten-headed demon form, and his conflict with Prince Rama is deeply ingrained in Sri Lankan culture and is celebrated in traditional dance, music, and drama.

The tale of Sita, the virtuous wife of Prince Rama, is also widely revered in Sri Lankan folklore. The story of her abduction by Ravana and her subsequent rescue by Prince Rama is a central theme in many folk traditions. The Ramayana has inspired numerous artistic interpretations, including traditional dance dramas such as the "Rama Seetha Ravana" performed in Sri Lanka.

Another popular legend in Sri Lankan folklore is the story of Kataragama Deviyo, a deity worshipped by both Sinhalese and Tamil communities. Kataragama Deviyo is believed to be a guardian deity associated with protection, fertility, and fulfillment of wishes. The annual Esala Perahera festival held in Kataragama, featuring grand processions and religious rituals, is a significant event where devotees pay homage to this revered deity.

The story of the demon princess Kuveni is another intriguing legend in Sri Lankan folklore. According to the ancient chronicles, Kuveni was a Yaksha princess who married the legendary King Vijaya, the first recorded king of Sri Lanka. The tale of their marriage, subsequent conflicts, and Kuveni's ultimate fate has captivated the imagination of Sri Lankans and serves as a cautionary tale about the consequences of intercultural encounters.

Folklore in Sri Lanka is not limited to ancient legends and epics but also includes a rich collection of tales featuring animals, spirits, and mythical creatures. The "Thovil" rituals, performed by exorcists known as "Kattadiyas," incorporate elements of animism and shamanism, drawing upon a diverse range of supernatural beings believed to influence human lives.

One famous mythical creature in Sri Lankan folklore is the "Yaksha," a supernatural being associated with natural elements such as mountains, forests, and rivers. Yakshas are depicted as powerful guardians or mischievous tricksters in folk tales, and their presence is believed to bring blessings or cause misfortune. The belief in Yakshas reflects the deep connection between the Sri Lankan people and the natural environment.

Sri Lanka's folklore is also rich in stories about legendary animals such as the "Garunda," a mythical bird with incredible strength and divine powers. The Garunda is often depicted in ancient Sri Lankan art and sculptures, symbolizing protection and victory.

In addition to mythical creatures, Sri Lankan folklore includes tales of benevolent spirits known as "Kinnaras" and "Nagas." Kinnaras are celestial beings associated with music, dance, and love, while Nagas are serpentine creatures believed to possess supernatural powers and guard hidden treasures. These tales add a touch of enchantment and mysticism to Sri Lanka's folklore tradition.

Folklore and legends serve multiple purposes in Sri Lankan society. They not only entertain and inspire imagination but also provide moral lessons, reinforce cultural values, and create a sense of shared identity. Through the retelling of these tales, Sri Lankans connect with their past, transmit cultural knowledge, and nurture a sense of belonging within their communities.

In conclusion, the folklore and legends of Sri Lanka form a captivating tapestry of myths, tales, and supernatural beings that reflect the cultural richness and diversity of the island. These stories have endured the test of time, carrying within them the wisdom, beliefs, and collective imagination of the Sri Lankan people.

# Sri Lankan Cuisine: A Delicious Fusion of Flavors

Sri Lankan cuisine is a culinary delight, offering a tantalizing fusion of flavors that reflects the country's diverse cultural influences and abundant natural resources. From aromatic spices to fresh tropical ingredients, this chapter explores the vibrant and mouthwatering world of Sri Lankan cuisine, highlighting its unique characteristics, traditional dishes, and the cultural significance of food in Sri Lankan society.

At the heart of Sri Lankan cuisine lies its incredible array of spices. The island's strategic location along ancient spice routes brought a multitude of flavors from around the world, including cinnamon, cardamom, cloves, nutmeg, and black pepper. These spices, often used in their whole form or freshly ground, lend depth and complexity to Sri Lankan dishes, creating a symphony of aromatic sensations.

One hallmark of Sri Lankan cuisine is the generous use of coconut in various forms. Coconut is a versatile ingredient that finds its way into curries, chutneys, sambols, and desserts. Coconut milk, made by grating the flesh and squeezing out the creamy liquid, forms the base of many Sri Lankan curries, lending them a rich and velvety texture. Grated coconut, both fresh and dried, adds texture and flavor to a variety of dishes.

Rice, the staple food of Sri Lanka, holds a central place in its culinary traditions. Sri Lankans consume rice with almost every meal, often complemented by a range of delectable side dishes. From fragrant biryanis to comforting rice and curry combinations, rice forms the foundation of many Sri Lankan meals and is a symbol of nourishment and sustenance.

Curries are an integral part of Sri Lankan cuisine and are bursting with bold flavors. Sri Lankan curries, unlike their Indian counterparts, tend to be spicier and hotter due to the generous use of chili peppers. The base for most curries is a mixture of onions, garlic, ginger, and a combination of roasted spices that create a depth of flavor. The curries feature an assortment of vegetables, meat, or seafood, each contributing its distinct taste to the dish.

One iconic Sri Lankan dish is "Hoppers" or "Appa," a type of pancake made from fermented rice flour and coconut milk. Hoppers are typically crispy on the edges and soft in the center, and they can be enjoyed plain or with an egg cracked into the center. String hoppers, a variation made from rice flour noodles, are another popular breakfast or dinner option, often served with coconut sambol or curry.

The vibrant and fiery "Sambols" of Sri Lanka add an explosion of flavor to any meal. These condiments, made with a variety of ingredients such as grated coconut, chili peppers, lime juice, and spices, are typically served alongside rice and curry. The most famous sambol is "Pol Sambol," a combination of freshly grated coconut, red chili flakes, lime juice, and onions, offering a delightful balance of heat, tanginess, and sweetness.

Seafood holds a special place in Sri Lankan cuisine due to the country's coastal location. From succulent prawns and crabs to a variety of fish species, Sri Lankans incorporate seafood into their culinary repertoire with flair. "Ambul

Thiyal," a tangy and spicy fish curry, and "Jaffna Prawn Curry," cooked in a rich blend of spices and coconut milk, are just a couple of examples that highlight the abundance of seafood dishes in Sri Lankan cuisine.

Sweets and desserts in Sri Lanka are a delightful finale to any meal or a treat enjoyed on special occasions. Traditional Sri Lankan sweets often feature jaggery, a type of unrefined sugar made from palm sap, and include treats such as "Kavum" (deep-fried sweetmeats), "Watalappan" (a rich coconut custard), and "Kiri Pani" (milk toffees). These sweet indulgences showcase the country's love for flavors like cardamom, cinnamon, and treacle.

The cultural significance of food in Sri Lankan society extends beyond mere sustenance. Meals are often communal affairs, bringing family and friends together. The act of sharing food is considered an expression of love, hospitality, and togetherness. Traditional Sri Lankan hospitality dictates that guests be treated with respect and offered a variety of dishes to choose from, creating a sense of warmth and belonging.

Sri Lankan cuisine is a result of centuries of cultural exchange and influence. The indigenous flavors, combined with the culinary contributions of Arab traders, Indian immigrants, and European colonizers, have shaped the unique character of Sri Lankan dishes. The country's culinary heritage is a testament to the resilience and adaptability of its people.

In recent years, Sri Lankan cuisine has gained international recognition for its bold flavors and diverse offerings. Restaurants around the world now feature Sri Lankan dishes, introducing global audiences to the richness of the country's culinary traditions. The availability of Sri Lankan ingredients and spices in international markets has further facilitated the exploration and appreciation of Sri Lankan cuisine beyond its shores.

In conclusion, Sri Lankan cuisine is a delectable fusion of flavors, spices, and ingredients that tantalize the taste buds and reflect the cultural diversity of the country. From aromatic curries to crispy hoppers and sweet indulgences, Sri Lankan food is a celebration of flavors and a testament to the country's culinary heritage.

# Gems of Sri Lanka: The Island's Rich Gemstone Industry

Sri Lanka, often referred to as the "Jewel Box of the Indian Ocean," has a long and storied history of gemstone mining and trading. Renowned for its exceptional gem deposits, the island has been a destination for gem enthusiasts and traders for centuries. This chapter delves into the world of Sri Lanka's gemstone industry, exploring the country's precious gems, their significance, mining techniques, and the global impact of Sri Lankan gemstones.

Sri Lanka is blessed with an abundance of gemstones, ranging from the illustrious Ceylon sapphires to vibrant rubies, dazzling emeralds, and a variety of semi-precious stones. The country's gem deposits are found in different regions, with Ratnapura, Elahera, and Metiyagoda being among the prominent gemstone mining areas. These regions are known for their rich mineral resources and have played a significant role in Sri Lanka's gemstone industry.

Ceylon sapphires, in particular, hold a special place in Sri Lanka's gemstone heritage. Known for their intense blue hues, Ceylon sapphires are highly valued for their clarity, brilliance, and color saturation. The gemstone industry in Sri Lanka has thrived on the production and export of Ceylon sapphires, which are sought after by jewelry connoisseurs worldwide.

Another notable gemstone found in Sri Lanka is the mesmerizing padparadscha sapphire. Renowned for its delicate pinkish-orange color, the padparadscha sapphire is considered one of the rarest and most coveted gemstones.

Sri Lanka is recognized as the traditional source for these exquisite stones, which are highly prized for their beauty and uniqueness.

The gemstone mining process in Sri Lanka combines traditional techniques with modern advancements. Artisanal miners, known as "Ratnaparikshaka," employ age-old methods such as panning in riverbeds, digging pits, and tunneling to extract gem-bearing gravels. Once the raw gem-bearing material is collected, it undergoes a process called "gem gravel washing," where it is carefully washed and sieved to separate the gemstones from the surrounding debris.

After the initial extraction, the gemstones go through a meticulous sorting and grading process. Skilled gemstone cutters and lapidaries transform the rough stones into exquisite gems by employing various cutting and polishing techniques. Sri Lankan lapidaries are renowned for their precision and craftsmanship, ensuring that the gemstones exhibit their optimal brilliance and beauty.

The Sri Lankan gemstone industry operates under a well-regulated framework to ensure the authenticity and quality of the gemstones. The National Gem and Jewelry Authority of Sri Lanka (NGJA) oversees the licensing, mining regulations, and ethical practices within the industry. The NGJA also works towards promoting sustainable mining practices and protecting the country's gemstone resources.

Sri Lankan gemstones have made a significant impact on the global market, with many finding their way into prestigious jewelry collections and gemstone auctions. The reputation of Sri Lankan gemstones for their exceptional quality and natural beauty has garnered international recognition and demand.

The gemstone industry in Sri Lanka contributes significantly to the country's economy, providing employment opportunities and generating foreign exchange through exports. Gemstone trading centers, such as Ratnapura and the capital city of Colombo, serve as hubs for gemstone buyers and traders from around the world. Sri Lanka's gemstone industry not only adds economic value but also showcases the country's rich geological heritage.

Ethical considerations in the Sri Lankan gemstone industry are gaining increasing importance. Efforts are being made to promote responsible mining practices, fair trade, and sustainability. Initiatives such as "Gemstone Ethical Trading Standard" and "Gemstone Good Governance Standard" aim to ensure that gemstone mining and trading uphold environmental and social standards.

In conclusion, Sri Lanka's gemstone industry is a treasure trove of remarkable gemstones that have captivated the world with their beauty and allure. From the renowned Ceylon sapphires to the elusive padparadscha sapphires, Sri Lankan gemstones have become synonymous with exceptional quality and natural splendor. The industry's rich history, skilled artisans, and commitment to ethical practices continue to position Sri Lanka as a prominent player in the global gemstone market.

# Tsunamis and Natural Disasters: Sri Lanka's Encounter with Nature's Fury

Sri Lanka, nestled in the Indian Ocean, has a history of encounters with natural disasters that have left a lasting impact on the island and its people. From devastating tsunamis to cyclones and floods, this chapter explores the country's experiences with nature's fury, highlighting the impact of these disasters, the response efforts, and the resilience of the Sri Lankan people.

Tsunamis, powerful ocean waves caused by undersea earthquakes, have had a profound effect on Sri Lanka. The most catastrophic event in recent history occurred on December 26, 2004, when a massive undersea earthquake off the coast of Sumatra triggered a tsunami that swept across the Indian Ocean. Sri Lanka was one of the hardest-hit countries, with the eastern and southern coastal regions bearing the brunt of the disaster.

The 2004 Indian Ocean tsunami caused widespread devastation along Sri Lanka's coastline. Entire communities were engulfed by the relentless force of the waves, resulting in the loss of thousands of lives, displacement of hundreds of thousands of people, and extensive damage to infrastructure. The tsunami's impact was felt across multiple sectors, including housing, transportation, healthcare, and the economy.

In the aftermath of the tsunami, Sri Lanka received international support and assistance to aid in recovery and reconstruction efforts. Humanitarian organizations, governments, and individuals from around the world rallied to provide emergency relief, including food, water, medical supplies, and shelter. The Sri Lankan government, along with local and international organizations, undertook a massive rehabilitation and reconstruction program to rebuild communities and restore livelihoods.

The 2004 tsunami was a wake-up call for Sri Lanka and highlighted the need for improved disaster preparedness and early warning systems. In response, the government, in collaboration with international partners, established the Disaster Management Center (DMC) to coordinate disaster response and mitigation efforts. The DMC focuses on disaster risk reduction, emergency response planning, and capacity-building to enhance the country's resilience to future disasters.

In addition to tsunamis, Sri Lanka is prone to other natural disasters, including cyclones and floods. The island's geographical location exposes it to the monsoon climate, which brings heavy rains during specific seasons. Cyclones originating in the Bay of Bengal can also cause significant damage, particularly to coastal areas. The impact of these disasters can result in loss of life, damage to infrastructure, disruption of essential services, and the displacement of communities.

Efforts to mitigate the impact of natural disasters in Sri Lanka are ongoing. The government, with the support of international organizations and community-based initiatives, has been working to improve early warning systems, strengthen disaster preparedness and response mechanisms, and enhance infrastructure resilience. These measures aim to minimize the loss of life and property and facilitate a more effective response during times of crisis.

Sri Lankans have demonstrated remarkable resilience in the face of natural disasters. Communities have come together to support each other, rebuild homes, and restore their lives. The spirit of volunteerism, unity, and solidarity has been instrumental in the recovery process and the rebuilding of affected areas.

It is essential to acknowledge that natural disasters are an inherent part of the earth's dynamics, and their occurrence cannot be completely prevented. However, proactive measures can be taken to reduce vulnerability, increase preparedness, and enhance resilience. Building stronger infrastructure, implementing early warning systems, educating communities about disaster preparedness, and promoting sustainable land-use practices are crucial steps in mitigating the impact of natural disasters.

In conclusion, Sri Lanka's encounters with tsunamis and other natural disasters have had a profound impact on the country and its people. The devastating consequences of these events have underscored the importance of disaster preparedness, early warning systems, and effective response mechanisms. Through collective efforts, Sri Lanka continues to strengthen its resilience and strive towards a safer and more resilient future.

# Modern Sri Lanka: The Journey to Economic Development and Global Integration

Sri Lanka's path to modernity has been marked by significant strides in economic development and global integration. This chapter explores the country's journey in recent times, highlighting its efforts to build a strong and diversified economy, foster international partnerships, and navigate the challenges and opportunities of the global stage. From policy reforms to infrastructure development and innovation, Sri Lanka has embraced a vision of progress and has made significant strides towards achieving its goals.

One key driver of Sri Lanka's economic development has been its commitment to open markets and international trade. The country has pursued a liberal trade policy, seeking to expand its export base and attract foreign investment. Sri Lanka's strategic location along major shipping routes and its membership in international trade agreements, such as the World Trade Organization (WTO), have provided avenues for increased trade and investment opportunities.

Sri Lanka's economy has experienced notable growth and diversification in recent years. The country has moved beyond traditional industries such as agriculture and tea production and has expanded into sectors such as information technology, tourism, apparel manufacturing, and services. These sectors have played a vital role in job creation, technology transfer, and boosting the country's overall economic growth.

Infrastructure development has been a crucial component of Sri Lanka's modernization efforts. The government has invested significantly in improving transportation networks, including the expansion of highways, modernizing ports, and upgrading airports. These infrastructure projects aim to enhance connectivity, facilitate trade and tourism, and attract foreign direct investment.

Education and skills development have also been prioritized as key drivers of economic growth. Sri Lanka places importance on its human capital, investing in education and vocational training to equip its workforce with the skills necessary to meet the demands of a rapidly changing global economy. The country has made significant progress in achieving high literacy rates and expanding access to quality education at various levels.

In recent years, Sri Lanka has sought to strengthen its ties with the international community through diplomatic engagement and participation in regional and global organizations. The country has actively engaged in forums such as the United Nations and has pursued partnerships with countries across the world. Sri Lanka's diplomatic efforts aim to foster collaboration, attract foreign investment, and create avenues for knowledge sharing and technology transfer.

Sri Lanka's tourism sector has experienced substantial growth, attracting visitors from around the world to explore its natural beauty, rich cultural heritage, and historical sites. The government has implemented measures to promote sustainable tourism practices, preserve natural ecosystems, and enhance the overall visitor experience. Tourism has emerged as a significant contributor to the country's economy and job creation.

Innovation and technology have played a crucial role in Sri Lanka's modernization journey. The country has fostered an environment conducive to innovation, entrepreneurship, and research and development. Sri Lanka's technology sector has witnessed notable growth, with the establishment of numerous tech startups and the emergence of vibrant tech hubs. These advancements have positioned Sri Lanka as a destination for innovation and a regional player in the technology industry. Challenges and opportunities coexist in Sri Lanka's journey towards economic development and global integration. The country continues to address issues such as income inequality, regional disparities, and environmental sustainability. Efforts are being made to promote inclusive growth, improve social welfare, and create an enabling environment for businesses to thrive.

Sri Lanka's commitment to sustainable development is evident in its efforts to protect the environment and natural resources. The country has implemented policies and initiatives to promote renewable energy, conservation of biodiversity, and sustainable agriculture practices. These measures reflect Sri Lanka's recognition of the importance of environmental stewardship in achieving long-term economic growth.

In conclusion, Sri Lanka's modernization journey is characterized by its commitment to economic development, global integration, and sustainable practices. Through strategic policies, infrastructure development, and international partnerships, the country is making significant progress in realizing its vision of a prosperous and inclusive nation. While challenges persist, Sri Lanka's resilience and determination position it to seize the opportunities of a rapidly changing global landscape.

# Conclusion

Throughout this book, we have explored the rich and vibrant history of Sri Lanka, delving into ancient civilizations, cultural milestones, colonial encounters, and the country's journey towards modernity. From the enchanting origins to the challenges and triumphs of the present, Sri Lanka's story is one of resilience, diversity, and cultural richness.

Sri Lanka, often referred to as the "Pearl of the Indian Ocean," has captivated the world with its natural beauty, historical heritage, and warm hospitality. The island's strategic location has made it a melting pot of cultures, with influences from India, Southeast Asia, the Arab world, and Europe leaving indelible imprints on its society, language, art, architecture, and cuisine.

Ancient Sri Lanka witnessed the rise and fall of magnificent kingdoms, the construction of remarkable architectural wonders, and the flourishing of art, literature, and spiritual traditions. The ancient cities of Anuradhapura, Polonnaruwa, and Sigiriya stand as testaments to the ingenuity and vision of past civilizations. The arrival of Buddhism from India brought profound changes to the religious and cultural landscape, shaping the ethos of Sri Lankan society.

The colonial era brought European influences and domination to the island, with the Portuguese, Dutch, and British leaving their mark on Sri Lanka's history. The impacts of colonization were both transformative and complex, shaping political systems, introducing new crops and industries, and leaving lasting legacies that continue to shape the country's social fabric.

Sri Lanka's journey to independence was marked by the awakening of national consciousness and the emergence of political leaders who fought for self-rule and the rights of the people. The country's post-independence era has witnessed efforts towards economic development, social progress, and the strengthening of democratic institutions. Sri Lanka has sought to carve a place for itself on the global stage, fostering international relationships and embracing the opportunities and challenges of the modern world.

The diverse ethnic, religious, and linguistic communities that call Sri Lanka home have contributed to its cultural tapestry and fostered a sense of unity amidst diversity. Sri Lanka's cultural revival efforts have celebrated traditional arts, crafts, and performing arts, preserving and revitalizing these cultural treasures for future generations.

Sri Lanka's journey has not been without challenges. The country has faced internal conflicts and ethnic tensions, which have had a profound impact on its society and development. Efforts towards reconciliation, inclusivity, and the pursuit of peace continue to be important aspects of Sri Lanka's journey towards a more harmonious and equitable society.

As we conclude this book, it is important to recognize that Sri Lanka's story is not static. It is a dynamic narrative that continues to unfold, shaped by the actions, aspirations, and resilience of its people. The future holds both opportunities and challenges, and it is the collective responsibility of Sri

Lankans, along with the support and engagement of the global community, to navigate the path ahead.

Sri Lanka's rich history, cultural heritage, natural beauty, and the warmth of its people make it a captivating destination. It is a country that invites exploration, appreciation, and understanding. By studying its history, we gain insights into its past, present, and future, and develop a deeper appreciation for the complexities of its society and the remarkable journey it has undertaken.

In closing, the history of Sri Lanka is a testament to the indomitable spirit of its people, their resilience in the face of adversity, and their commitment to preserving and celebrating their cultural heritage. As we bid farewell to this exploration of Sri Lanka's past, let us carry forward the lessons learned and the appreciation gained, fostering a deeper understanding of this remarkable island nation.

Dear Reader,

Thank you for embarking on this journey through the pages of "The History of Sri Lanka." We sincerely hope that you found the book enlightening, engaging, and informative. Your commitment to exploring the rich history, culture, and natural wonders of Sri Lanka is truly appreciated.

We understand that your time and attention are valuable, and we are grateful that you chose to invest them in this book. Our aim was to provide you with an authentic and captivating exploration of Sri Lanka's past, present, and future, and we hope that we have succeeded in doing so.

If you enjoyed reading "The History of Sri Lanka" and found it to be a valuable resource, we kindly request that you consider leaving a positive review. Your feedback will not only help us improve our work but also encourage other readers to discover and delve into the fascinating world of Sri Lanka's history.

Your support means a great deal to us, and we are grateful for the opportunity to share our passion for Sri Lanka with you. We hope that this book has deepened your understanding of the country and its remarkable journey through the ages.

Once again, thank you for joining us on this literary adventure. We look forward to continuing to provide you with insightful and captivating stories in the future.

Printed in Great Britain
by Amazon